To
Hannah,

Saw this and thought of you.
I hope it enhances your
wonderful creativity and I
look forward to seeing the
results. You're fab!
Lots of love

Stef x

SKETCHING
└→TYPE

CREATE YOUR OWN HAND-DRAWN TYPE

SKETCHING TYPE

FREEHAND THIS WAY→

TYP SKETCH DRAW PENCIL·PEN

LEE SUTTEY

Sketching Type
Author: Lee Suttey

First published in Great Britain in 2016 by Mitchell Beazley,
an imprint of Octopus Publishing Group Ltd,
Carmelite House, 50 Victoria Embankment, London EC4Y 0DZ
www.octopusbooks.co.uk

An Hachette UK Company
www.hachette.co.uk

ISBN: 978 1 78472 123 7

Set in Thurston and Interstate

Printed and bound in China

Conceived, designed and produced by
Quid Publishing
Part of the Quarto Group
Level 4 Sheridan House
Hove BN3 1DD
England

Design and illustration: Lee Suttey, Visual Function_

BIG THANKS

TO MY WIFE EMMA AND OUR BABY DAUGHTER MATILDA
FOR BEARING WITH ME WHEN WORKING WEEKENDS IN
MY STUDIO AND TO JAMES FOR HAVING THE FAITH IN ME
TO WRITE MY FIRST BOOK.

6

CONTENTS

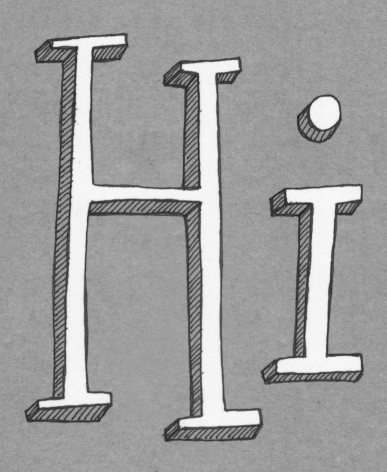

INTRODUCTION

THIS BOOK IS FOR ANYONE WHO LOVES TYPE AND LOVES TO DOODLE, SKETCH AND DRAW. IT'S PACKED WITH INSPIRATIONAL EXERCISES TO INSPIRE YOUR CREATIVITY AND HELP YOU GET STARTED.

SKETCHING TYPE DOESN'T REQUIRE TOO MUCH KNOWLEDGE OF TYPOGRAPHY, ALTHOUGH IT HELPS TO KNOW THE RULES BEFORE YOU START BREAKING THEM. IN EACH SECTION YOU'LL FIND NOTES ON THE CHARACTERISTICS AND ANATOMY OF THE TYPE STYLE IN QUESTION, ALONG WITH SKETCHED EXAMPLES AND IDEAS. THERE ARE ALSO SPECIAL GUEST SPOTS THROUGHOUT, GIVING INSIGHTS FROM A SELECTION OF EXPERTS IN THE FIELD. AT THE BACK OF THE BOOK YOU'LL FIND SUGGESTIONS ON HOW TO USE YOUR HAND-DRAWN CREATIONS.

COMPUTERS HAVE MADE IT MUCH EASIER TO MANIPULATE TYPE, BUT HAVING A PENCIL AND A BLANK PIECE OF PAPER GIVES YOU EVEN MORE OF A CHALLENGE. THERE IS SOMETHING ABOUT HAND-DRAWN TYPE THAT IS VERY HARD TO REPLICATE DIGITALLY, WHICH IS WHAT MAKES IT SO UNIQUE!

LET'S SKETCH SOME TYPE

WHAT YOU WILL NEED

Here are a few essentials you'll need for creating your hand-drawn type:

EYES

You can find hand-drawn type on signs, posters, books, windows and walls, so look for inspiration whenever you're out and about.

IMAGINATION

This is obviously one of your most valuable creative tools. Before you start sketching, visualise your type and focus on what you're aiming to achieve and the best way to go about it.

PENCIL

This one kind of goes without saying, as this book is about sketching. The benefit of starting your type in pencil is that you'll quickly see if it's going to work, without spending too much of your time labouring over the detail.

SHARPENER

It sounds simple, but using a sharp pencil helps to keep your lines clear and crisp. Not only will this make your pencil work look more finished, it'll also help if you want to redraw your letters in ink.

ERASER

If you're new to sketching type, it's bound to take some time for you to get your technique down – and you'll always want to tweak your designs. So having a good eraser is essential.

PENS

Using a pen to fill in the detail and finish off your pencil-drawn type can transform the way it looks. I would also recommend using just a pen every now and then – it's a nice challenge, as you have to stick with the first marks you make.

PAPER

This book uses a variety of paper styles – plain, lined, grid-lined, etc. Consider how this can give your type a different feel, and see if you prefer drawing using one style over another.

HANDS

These come in handy.

PRACTICE

They say practice makes perfect, and it's no different with hand-drawn type. The pages in this book are designed to help you develop new ideas and styles and hone your type-drawing skills. This is especially useful if you're thinking of putting your type to use outside of the confines of these pages.

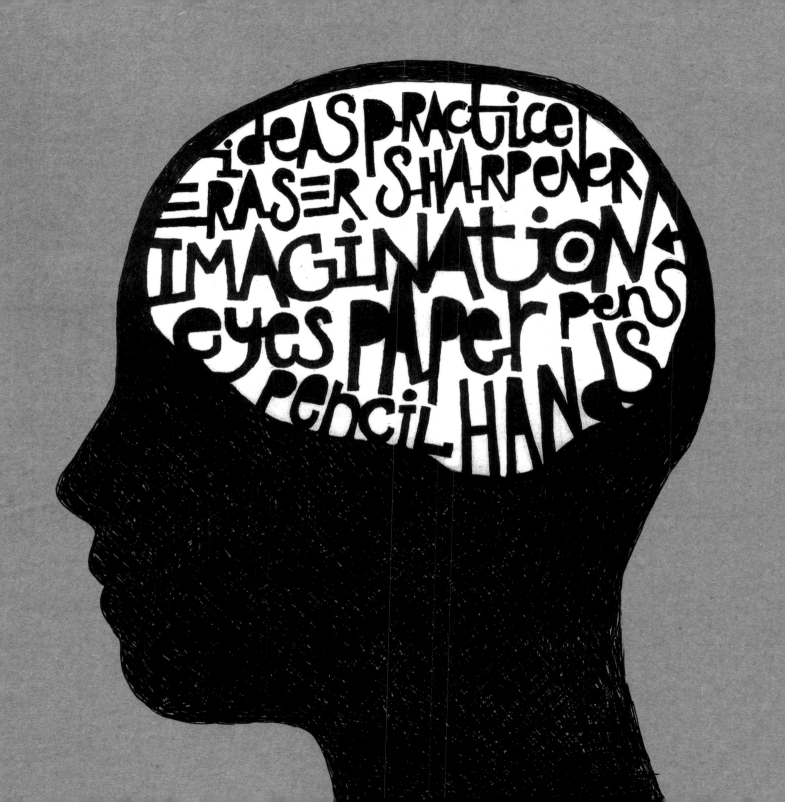

GETTING STARTED

Before you get sketching, take a look at the basic pointers below:

There is no right or wrong way when drawing type; it depends on your idea and what you're trying to achieve. Generally, though, I'd recommend starting off by sketching out your letters roughly with a single pencil line. This will give you a basic framework to develop.

You can see in the stages above how I worked on my name, adding decoration and changing the thickness of the line as I developed the type. I find that once you start drawing you get a sense of what styles and details will suit the letters.

THINKING ABOUT YOUR APPROACH

As the letters in my name lend themselves well to being joined up, I wanted to draw the type with one continuous line. Look at your word (or words) before you put pencil to paper, to see if there's an obvious way to make your hand-drawn type work.

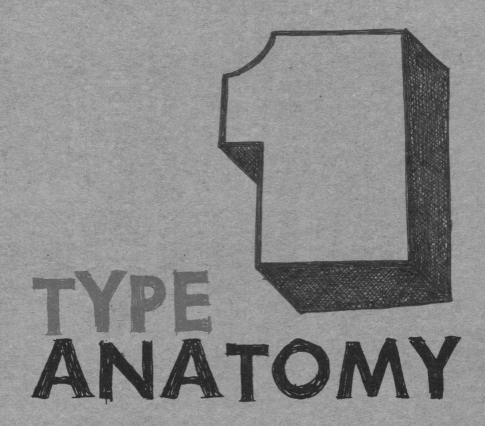

TYPE
ANATOMY

THIS SECTION WILL COVER THE BASICS OF TYPE ANATOMY, TO GET YOU FAMILIAR WITH THE CONSTITUENT PARTS OF LETTERS (THE SMALL DETAILS THAT GIVE TYPE ITS CHARACTER), AND OFFER AN ESSENTIAL FIRST LESSON IN TYPE-SKETCHING SKILLS.

COUNTER-LESS TYPE

In typography, the counter is the area of blank space that is enclosed, either entirely or partially, by the rest of the letterform – the hole in an 'o', for example.

A counter is also known as the inner or enclosed space. The term 'counter' is generally only used to refer to enclosed spaces, whereas partially enclosed spaces – found in letters such as 'm' and 'n' – are referred to as open counters or apertures.

Below you'll find a couple of sketched examples of counter-less type...

COUNTER-LESS CHARACTERS

LETTERS CONTAINING CLOSED COUNTERS INCLUDE:
A, B, D, O, P, Q, R, a, b, d, e, g, o, p and q

LETTERS CONTAINING OPEN COUNTERS (APERTURES) INCLUDE:
c, e, f, h, m, n, s and u

NUMBERS CONTAINING CLOSED COUNTERS:
0, 4, 6, 8 and 9

COUNTER TO COUNTER-LESS
On this letter, you can see the counter has been filled in. This style of 'a' is known as double-storey, since it has a counter at the bottom and an open counter at the top. The counter in the letter 'e' is called an eye.

APERTURE TO APERTURE-LESS
On this letter you can see I have lost the apertures, giving it a blocky, minimalistic feel.

**TRY CREATING YOUR OWN
COUNTER-LESS CHARACTERS**

SUN

↓ COUNTER

pattern

26

1 2 3 4
5 6 7 8
9 10

TYPE PALINDROME

aperture

HELLO

LISTEN

learn

ART

OPEN COFFEE

create ABSTRACT

WHY NOT TRY...

Filling in your counter spaces with a pattern?

b

4 Q

guard PROVERBS 4:23

YOUR HEART

ASCENDERS AND DESCENDERS

These are very common typographic terms: the ascender is the part of a character that extends up from the main body of the letter, such as the head on a 't'. The descender is the part of the character that extends below the main body of the letter, such as the tail on a 'y'.

The size of the main body of a letter is described by the term 'x-height' (literally the height of the lowercase 'x' in a given typeface). In the examples on this page, the ascenders and descenders are highlighted in blue.

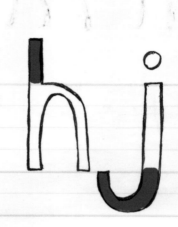

A DOT IS NOT AN ASCENDER

The dot on a 'j' or 'i' is called a tittle or superscript dot.

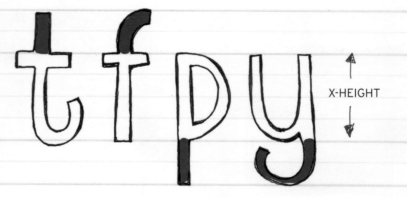

X-HEIGHT

ASCENDER CHARACTERS:
b, d, f, h, k, l, t

DESCENDER CHARACTERS:
g, j, p, q, y, (sometimes a capital J)

**TRY DRAWING YOUR OWN
ASCENDERS AND DESCENDERS**

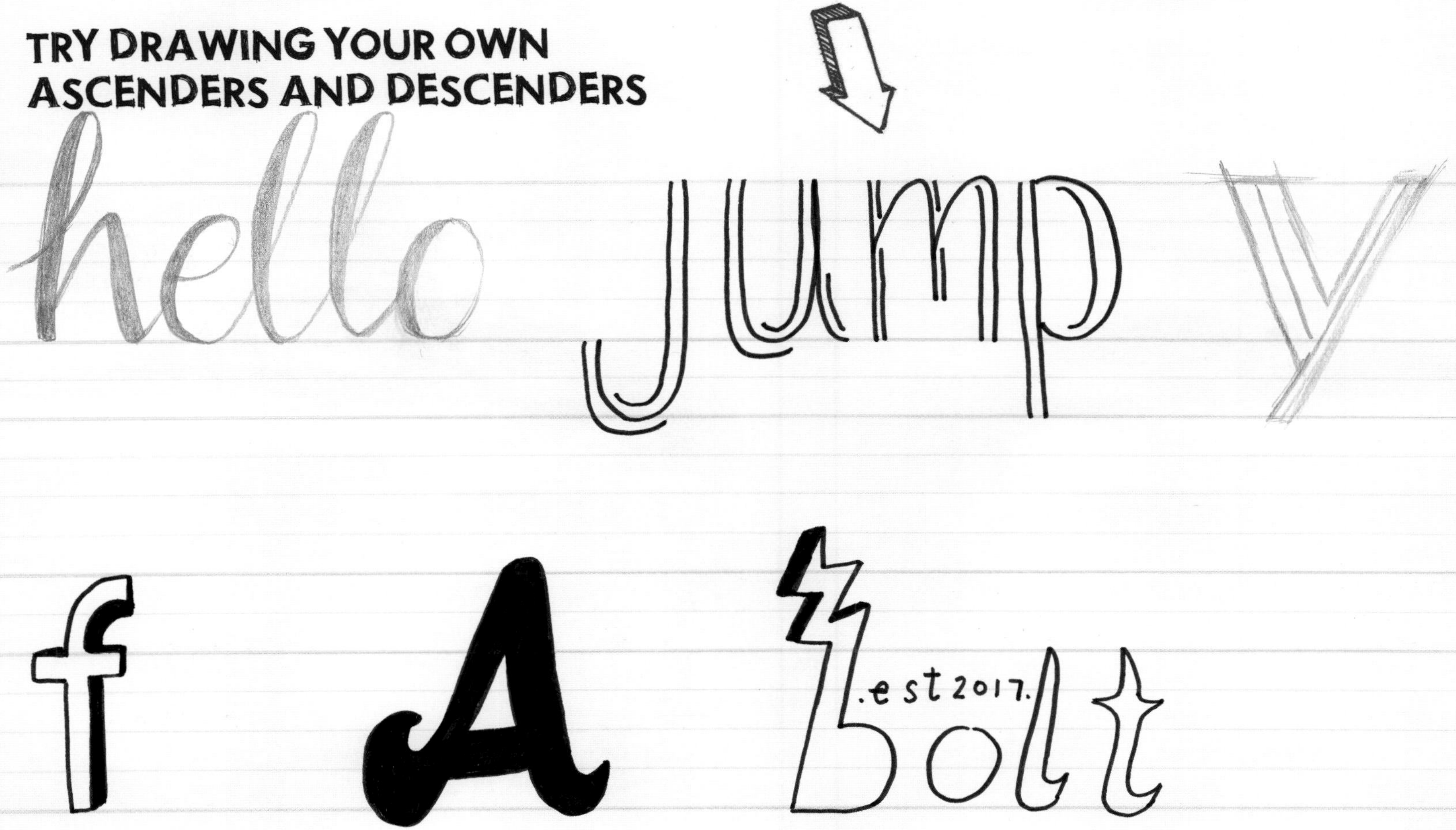

hello

jump

y

f

A

bolt

est 2017.

X-HEIGHT

USE THIS STYLE WHEN...

You want to ensure legibility in your type. That said, you can experiment with different kinds of ascenders and descenders – straight ones give a utilitarian feel, while exaggerated curly ones suggest elegance.

LINKED LETTERS (LIGATURES)

Linking letters is a nice way to give a piece of type a distinctive look. The typographic term for when two or more letters are joined to become a single character (technically a 'glyph') is 'ligature'.

It's common to see a ligature used when 'f' precedes another letter: 'fi', 'fl' and 'ff'. An ampersand (see page 164) is probably the most famous ligature, but because of its ubiquity it is no longer referred to as a ligature but as a logogram. It was created to combine the letters 'e' and 't', forming the word 'et' – Latin for 'and'.

Although ligatures in typesetting were introduced as a convenient way of printing two letters at once, they can be used with random letters to make something new and interesting.

A common set of ligatures

WHAT ARE GLYPHS?

'Glyph' is the technical term for the individual characters and symbols that make up a typeface. You can get more than one glyph style for a character in some typefaces.

WHAT ARE LOGOGRAMS?

These are specific symbols or glyphs that represent a word or phrase, for example: &, %, £, $, @.

TRY LINKING UP YOUR LETTERS AND CREATING YOUR OWN LIGATURES

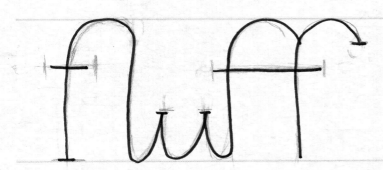

WHY NOT TRY...

Creating a word that is completely connected by ligatures?

USE THIS STYLE WHEN...
You want to add some subtle complexity
or individual quirks to your type.

ARTE

CRANK IT UP

Capital letters, also known as uppercase, are mainly used for headings or emphasis in typography (and for shouting in emails or blogs).

The term 'uppercase' comes from the way individual letters were stored and organised when printers set type by hand. The capital letters were stored in drawers, in a wooden box called a typecase, and this case was typically placed above the 'lowercase' letter drawers - hence 'upper' and 'lower' case.

When drawing your own uppercase letters, why not try to give them some character that reflects the type style. The letters I've drawn below emphasise the simplicity and larger size associated with uppercase letters.

LETTERS IN A TYPECASE

ALSO KNOWN AS:

Capital letters
Capitals
Caps
Large letters
Majuscule

**TRY DRAWING YOUR OWN
UPPERCASE ALPHABET**

A B C D E F G H I

J K L M

BRING IT DOWN

Smaller, non-capital letters are known as 'lowercase'. Unlike uppercase, in typography this style is often used for body text as its letterforms are softer on the eye. However, you can use it to create some really interesting hand-drawn type.

Like 'uppercase' (see page 28), the term 'lowercase' originates from the days of manual typesetting. Due to the fact that the smaller, lowercase letters were used more frequently than the larger, uppercase ones, the typecase they were stored in was lower down, nearer to the typesetter.

(see page 28)

ALSO KNOWN AS:
Small letters
Minuscule

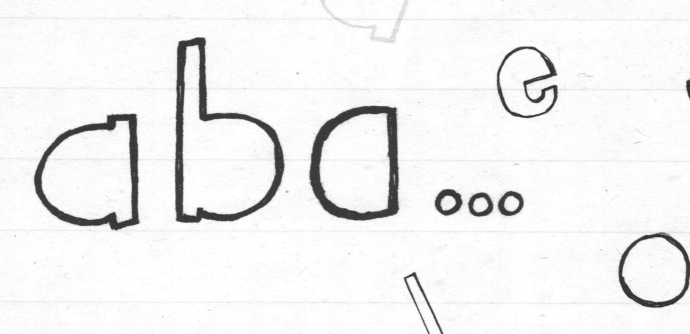

TRY DRAWING YOUR OWN LOWERCASE ALPHABET

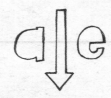

WHY NOT TRY...

Adding some features that reflect the 'low' nature of lowercase, like my 'l' arrow.

t2...

USE THIS STYLE WHEN...

You're sketching a long phrase or sentence, as it can help the legibility. It also works well as a distinctive style treatment for titles.

THICK AND THIN

The weight of the line (stroke thickness) of a typeface helps give the characters their characteristics!

Terms for stroke thickness were traditionally used to differentiate fonts within typeface families – 'bold' being an obvious example. However, there is no set standard for classifying a weight, so, as you're the designer of your hand-drawn type, you choose!

In the example below, the different line weights help emphasise the meaning of the word...

SOME WEIGHT CLASSIFICATIONS
→ Thin
→ Light
→ Roman
→ Medium
→ Bold
→ Black*
→ Ultra Black*

* These terms are used when you want a character that's bolder than bold!

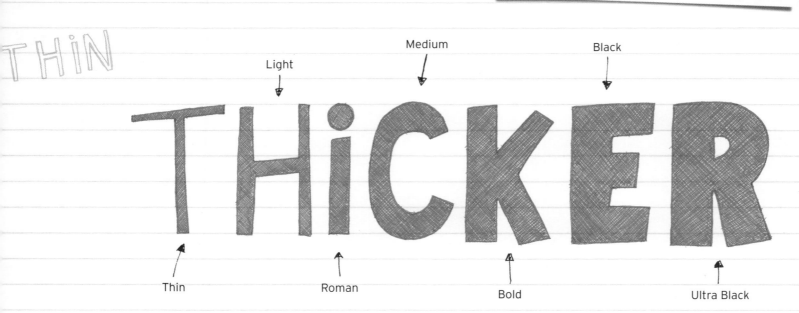

TRY DRAWING YOUR OWN WORDS WITH THICK AND THIN CHARACTERS

WHY NOT TRY...
Creating complete alphabets with various weights?

BOLD

ROMAN

USE THIS STYLE WHEN...
You want more variety! Different weights exist in typefaces to give the designer more flexibility when setting type - using the same style but in different weights gives coherence to your type.

THIN

KERNING AND LEADING

Good typography is really all about the spacing between the letters and lines, and how the type sits within a certain space.

'Kerning' is the term used for the adjustments a typesetter can make to the space between letters, and 'leading' is the term used for the vertical line spacing when type is set.

To the right you will see that I have drawn type *without* space between the letters. The great thing about sketching type is that the rules can be broken with real success, and you can begin to create your own visual style.

WHERE DID THE TERM 'LEADING' COME FROM?

Traditionally, before computers came along, metal typesetting used strips of lead to create variations to the space between the lines of type, hence 'leading'.

Today, leading is also known as line spacing, line feed and interlinear space. The authors among you might be familiar with the last term.

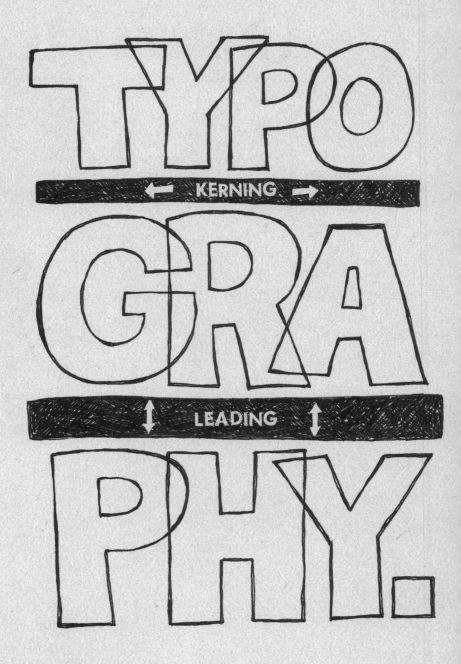

TRY DRAWING SOME OF YOUR TYPE
BUNCHEDUP OR S P A C E D O U T

KERNING

LEADING

These fixed guides will help you with consistency when you're exploring how kerning and leading can work.

CROSSING THE T'S

You can really go to town with making your hand-drawn type as individual as you are, by creating variations of the small details in your characters.

Below I've created a hand-drawn font called Time 74, which took inspiration from my signature, where I double cross my 't's (see right). A signature is a very personal and distinctive piece of type we all make without much thought.

In typography, the term 'cross stroke' refers to the single stroke that intersects the stem of a 't' or 'f'. In a capital 'A' and 'H', the cross stroke is known as a 'crossbar'. As you can see below with Time 74, I play with both and add them to each character.

my signature

ABCDEFGHIJKLMN
OPQRSTUVWXYZ

**TRY PLAYING WITH CROSS BARS
AND CROSS STROKES**

PLAYING WITH TYPE ANATOMY
Try combining or changing parts of your type's anatomy to create new styles for your hand-drawn type.

CARL FREDRIK

Carl Fredrik, aka 'Frisso', is a Norwegian graphic designer living in Copenhagen, Denmark.

While attending Kolding School of Design in Denmark, he went to Boston for a three-month apprenticeship with Josh Luke and Meredith Kasabian of Best Dressed Signs, to learn the craft of sign painting. Taking what he has learned, Carl is trying to make his mark on the visual landscapes of Oslo and Copenhagen by bringing hand-painted signage back to the cities, and bring hand-lettering to graphic design.

www.frisso151.com

TRY OUT YOUR OWN PAINTED SIGN TYPE ON THE NEXT PAGE

CARL'S APPROACH

In this hand-painted sign project, Carl has added a subtle detail to the links in his 'R's – a small but effective way of adding character with type anatomy. He says: 'When I'm making a sign, I always start off by sketching out the layout. Once the layout is in place and the lettering design is finished, I draw the design on to paper (scaled to the size of the sign board) to make the pounce pattern. The pattern is made by using a pouncewheel that pokes tiny holes in the paper as it traces the outlines. This way I can place the pattern on top of the primed sign board and gently punch chalk powder through the holes. When the pattern is removed, it leaves a trace of the chalk on the surface, outlining the design. Then I'm ready to bring out the brushes!'

CARL FREDRIK [49]

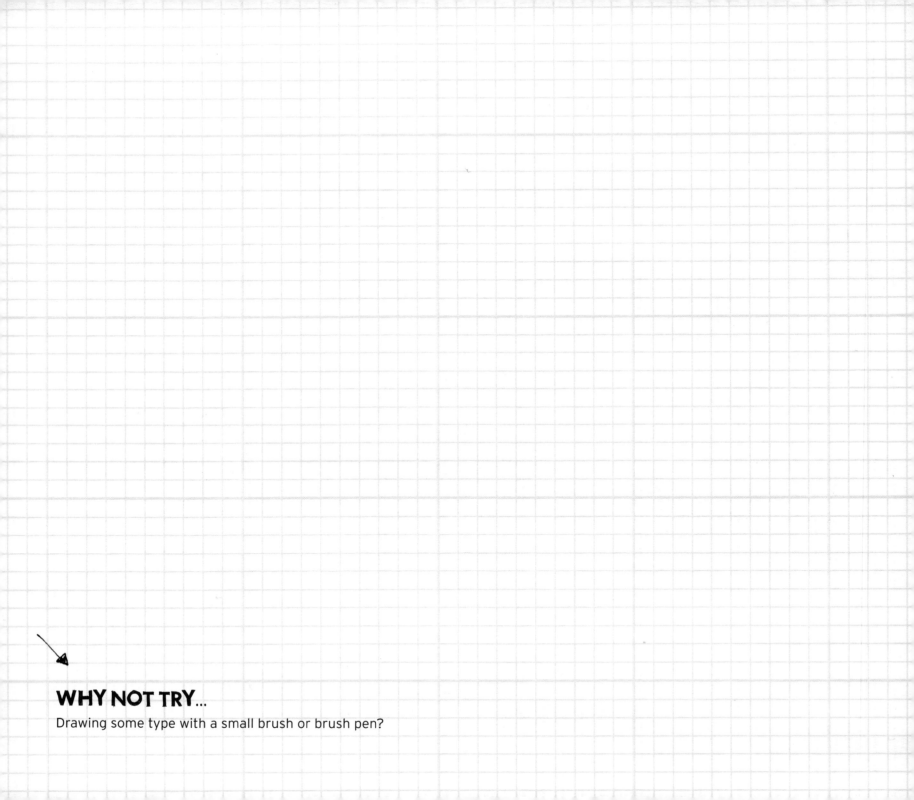

WHY NOT TRY...
Drawing some type with a small brush or brush pen?

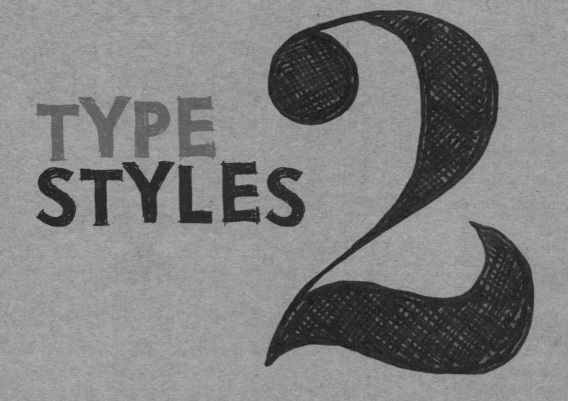

THIS SECTION LOOKS AT HOW
ESTABLISHED TYPE STYLES CAN BE
USED AS HANDY STARTING POINTS
FOR YOUR OWN STYLES.

ONCE YOU'RE FAMILIAR WITH
THE CLASSICS, YOU CAN CREATE
YOUR OWN.

SERIF TYPE

Serif type is distinct in that it has projecting features at the ends of the stems or strokes of the characters. 'Serif', from the Dutch *schreef*, means 'dash' or 'line'.

Serif type is traditionally considered easier to read than sans serif, which is why you find it widely used in large blocks of body copy in newspapers, novels and magazines. There are various shapes of serifs you can use: cupped, wedge, hairline and bracketed are just some of the options (check out the examples on pages 56-57).

You can draw and customise existing typefaces with serifs, or jump in with your own versions like I have on the right. Each of these examples uses thick, block-like slab serifs.

Times New Roman is one of the most popular seriffed typefaces, originally developed for *The Times* newspaper. It's a bit narrower than other similar serif fonts and allows more text to fit on a line, which is ideal for newspaper columns.

It is a transitional serif typeface, meaning the style is between the classifications of Old Style and Contemporary.

TRY DRAWING SOME OF YOUR OWN SERIF TYPE

Serif

WHY NOT TRY...

Combining your serifs with ligatures (see page 24)?

Serif
BRACKETED SERIF

serif
WEDGE SERIF

Serif

CUPPED SERIF

Serif

HAIRLINE SERIF

SANS SERIF TYPE

As opposed to serif type, a sans serif typeface has no projecting features on its stems and strokes. *Sans* in French means 'without', hence sans serif is 'without serif'.

The sans serif style is newer than the serif style, and has a more modern, clean feel. As you can see below, I have created a hand-drawn version of a very well-known sans serif font called Helvetica. I have used a thick, rough stroke, rather than a solid fill. You can add other style elements as you start to play around with yours – maybe take out some counters or add a ligature, for example...

helvetica

Helvetica is probably one of the most ubiquitous fonts out there – you'll see it everywhere once you start looking.

There has even been a film made about it called *Helvetica*, directed by Gary Hustwit. It was released in 2007 to celebrate the font's 50th birthday.

It's really worth checking out if you are interested in typography and want to find out more about the history of this iconic typeface.

**TRY DRAWING SOME
EXISTING SANS SERIF TYPE**

DIN
GILL SANS
VAG ROUNDED

These are just some of the sans serif
type styles you can use for inspiration.

GEOMETRIC SANS SERIF TYPE

Geometric type is most often created from regular circular, square or triangular shapes, with horizontal and vertical strokes that are of equal weight (i.e. a consistent line weight). Great for use in headings, due to its simplicity.

This style of type is ideal for giving your words a graphic feel and also lends itself really well to being drawn with a three-dimensional effect.

You can start by drawing circles, squares and triangles, and then begin to take away sections within the shapes like I have below.

Futura is one of the most common geometric sans serif typefaces. A very modern-looking font, even though it was designed in 1927!

It makes great use of simple geometric proportions and shapes, which creates a very clean feel.

Futura is influenced by the Bauhaus design style (see page 104).

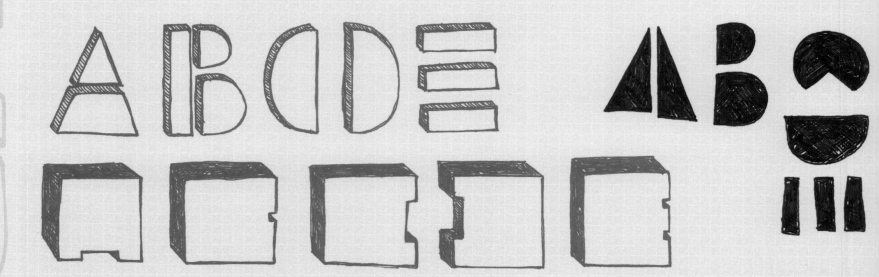

TRY DRAWING SOME OF
YOUR OWN GEOMETRIC TYPE

WHY NOT TRY...

Seeing how minimal you can make your
characters, while keeping the legibility?

USE THIS STYLE WHEN...

You want to keep things simple and to the point.
Avoid adding extra styling if this is the case.

STUNNING SCRIPTS

Script typefaces on computers often have a free-flowing feel to them. They're slanted with joined-up letters to emulate a hand-written style.

You will have seen this lettering used on things like invitations, because it's elegant and personal. You can really start to get elaborate with script styles, especially when hand-drawing them. Adding detail to your script type can change how it looks, such as in the three stages of my 'hello' example.

TRY DRAWING SOME OF
YOUR OWN STUNNING SCRIPTS

➤

WHY NOT TRY...

Digitally scanning your hand-drawn
scripts, and then experimenting with your
favourite image manipulation software?

OLD-STYLE NUMERALS

These are numbers designed using ascenders and descenders, i.e. they have parts that fall below and rise above the limits of the x-height (see page 20).

They are also known as non-lining figures, due to their irregular ascending and descending features.

With my '123' on the right, I've drawn very traditional-looking numbers capped with circles (ball terminals) rather than a serif or square end. The full set of numbers below uses a less formal style of character while adhering to the way old-style numerals work, i.e. using ascenders and descenders.

TRY DRAWING SOME OF YOUR OWN OLD-STYLE NUMERALS

WHY NOT TRY...

Incorporating old-style numerals into one of your type styles?

USE THIS STYLE WHEN…

You want to be more expressive with your numbers. You don't need to do maths with your hand-drawn numerals, so there is no need for them to line up neatly!

MONOSPACED

Monospaced type is designed so that each character fills a set width and was originally used in typewriters. Each letter on the typewriter keyboard operates a striker arm of a fixed width, which passes through the positioning gap and impresses onto the paper.

Monospaced type is also preferred for source code in computer programming - the regular spacing and characters make it easier to spot errors on screen. Many text editors have a monospaced typeface set as default for the same reason.

Think about the space around the letters when drawing your monospaced type - you might find it helpful to mark out your fixed width by drawing a grid or a line of regular shapes (or use the readymade one opposite). I've used typewriter keys to fix the space around the letters on the right, which adds an extra stylistic treatment.

TYPEWRITER STRIKER ARMS

COURIER TYPEWRITER FONT

Aa Bb Cc Dd Ee Ff
Gg Hh Ii Jj Kk Ll
Mm Nn Oo Pp Qq Rr
Ss Tt Uu Vv Ww Xx
Yy Zz=+2345678
9"/%&()!_.?,

TRY DRAWING SOME OF
YOUR OWN MONOSPACED TYPE

MONOSPACED {75}

USE THIS STYLE WHEN...

You want a rigid and regimented feel to your type. Combinations of monospaced character styles can also work together, if you feel the need to free things up a bit.

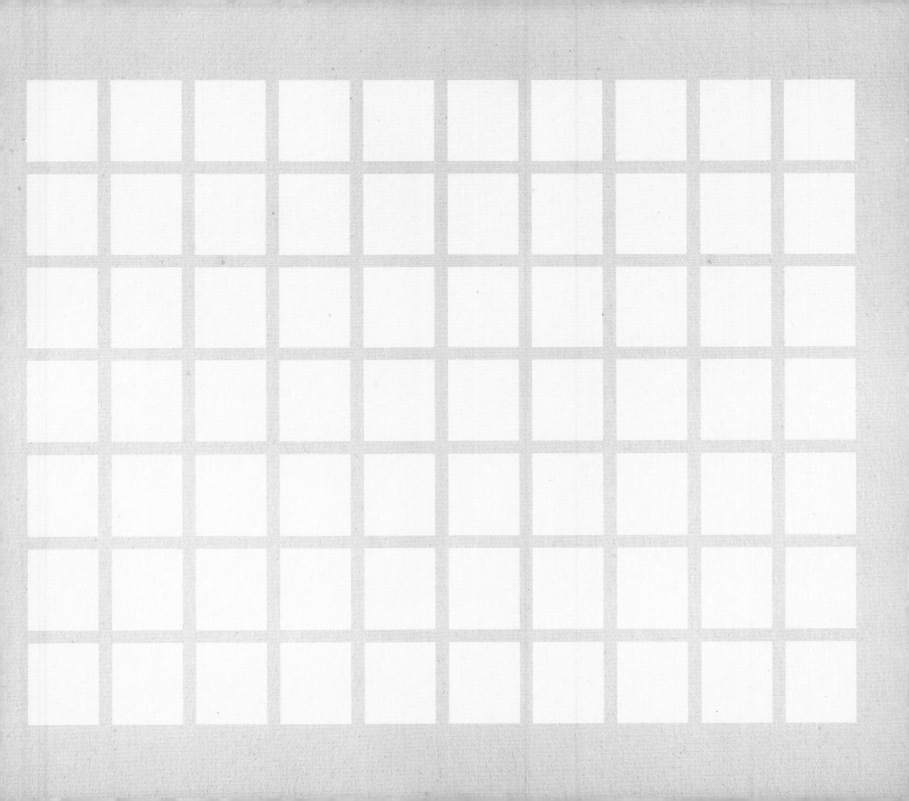

DINGBATS

These ornamental characters and symbols are not usually included in a standard typeface and are generally only used for decoration or emphasis. Their function, like their name, is a little playful.

You might have seen and used Zapf Dingbats on your Mac or PC; there is also Webdings, a set created for web use by Microsoft in 1997.

You can start to create hand-drawn dingbats to complement your developing type styles. Maybe even combine words and symbols like I have with my one-eyed dingbat.

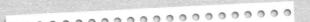

DID YOU KNOW?

If you type in 'NYC', the acronym for New York City, using the font Webdings, the three glyphs shown will be an eye, a heart and a city skyline: I love New York! (👁❤🏙)

TRY DRAWING SOME OF YOUR OWN DINGBATS

WHY NOT TRY...
Adding dingbats into the counters of some of your type?

SWASHES

In typography, a swash is a decorative stroke added to a letter – like an exaggerated serif (see page 54). The style dates back to 16th-century handwriting.

Below you can see the word 'Swash' with a lot of swashes! It's unfinished, as I am wondering if I can get a few more in there before I begin to do the final pen work.

DROP CAP?

A swash lends itself nicely to being used as a drop cap (see page 156).

TRY DRAWING SOME OF
YOUR OWN LETTERS WITH SWASHES

USE THIS STYLE WHEN...

You want to exaggerate a word and give it some traditional flair. Keep your word short and sweet to make things easier for yourself!

MARGARET CUSACK

Margaret Cusack is an illustrator, graphic designer and folk artist all in one.

Her work is best described as 'realism created with stitchery and fabric'. It is rich with colour, texture and detail, made with machine-appliqué and hand embroidery. Since 1972, she has created architectural-scale hangings, soft sculpture, portraits and props. Her stitched artwork has illustrated greeting cards, decorative plates, ads, posters, magazines, billboards and even postage stamps – all in fabric.

www.margaretcusack.com

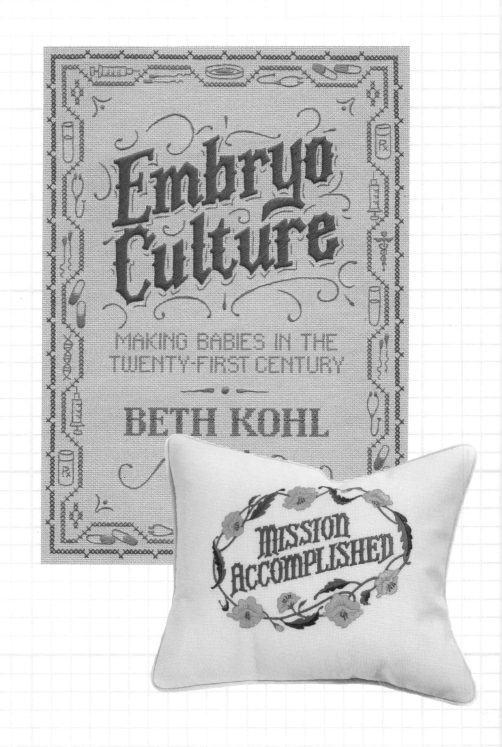

Embryo Culture

MAKING BABIES IN THE TWENTY-FIRST CENTURY

BETH KOHL

MISSION ACCOMPLISHED

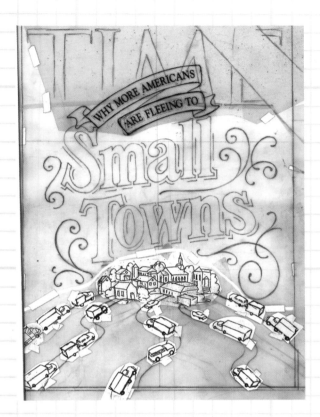

TRY OUT YOUR OWN STITCH-INSPIRED TYPE ON THE NEXT PAGE

MARGARET'S APPROACH

Margaret was commissioned to create stitched artwork for *Time* magazine. She sketched her main title type with cupped slab serifs, added a ball terminal to the 'a' in 'Small' and brought her 'T' below the lower x-height limit, giving the type a traditional but somewhat folksy style. These letters were then cut from cloth and hand-stitched onto textured white fabric.

Margaret says: 'I am always asked: "Why fabric?" The simple answer is: I am attuned to fabric's textures, patterns, and colours.'

WHY NOT TRY...

Drawing some type using short, horizontal lines,
to imitate the style of embroidery stitches?

RETRO
TYPE **3**

THE LOOK AND FEEL OF TYPE HAS
CHANGED DRASTICALLY OVER
THE YEARS, DUE TO TRENDS AND
TECHNOLOGICAL DEVELOPMENTS,
AMONG OTHER THINGS.

THIS SECTION LOOKS BACK OVER
SOME DISTINCTIVE PERIODS
IN HISTORY FOR TYPE INSPIRATION.

GOTHIC

In typography, the term 'Gothic' is often used when referring to blackletter type. Blackletter is a style of script that originated in the Middle Ages.

Blackletter is a calligraphic style, meaning the letter strokes are often sharply tapered and angular. There might also be breaks or thin connections at various points in the letterforms.

Due to the elaborate nature of this style, it's great for adding illustrative detail to individual letters. Use different angular lines for fills and add swirls to finish off the swashes (see page 82) as I have with my initials 'LS' below.

BLACKLETTER IN USE

Due to its distinctive look, blackletter can work well for logos and headings. It's authoritative, decorative and rock 'n' roll!

Newspapers such as *The Daily Telegraph* in the UK and *The New York Times* in the US, among many others, use it. The logo of heavy-metal band Motörhead uses it, and you can see it on many traditional European beer bottles. It's also often seen on people, as it's a very popular style of type for tattoos!

1 Start with calligraphy-style letters

3 Finish your type with a fill and some extra ornate decorations

2 Add some swashes and connecting lines

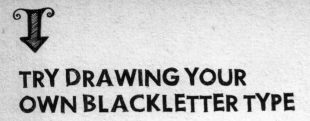

TRY DRAWING YOUR
OWN BLACKLETTER TYPE

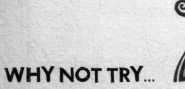

WHY NOT TRY...

Sketching some numbers in the Gothic style?

OLD AND NEW

You can draw a modern-looking character and then start adding some Gothic-style decoration as you work it up.

1

2

3

4

5

USE THIS STYLE WHEN...
You want to get really detailed with
your type. Got a calligraphy pen?
This style of type was made for it!

1800s

During the 1800s, ornate design trends became a major influence on typography and lettering design – you can see this by looking at advertisements of the time.

The type styles of this era were based on traditional letterforms, then embellished with shadows, outlines and other decorations. You can still see this style of lettering in hand-drawn signs and in product advertisements on the side of old buildings. These are known as ghost signs – see right – and it's always a treat when you spot one!

Nineteenth-century signage always makes me think of etching-style drawings of hands, pointing people in the right direction…

GHOST SIGNS

TRY DRAWING SOME OF YOUR OWN 19TH-CENTURY SIGN TYPE

WHY NOT TRY...

Sketching a modern-day advert in 1800s' style?

THIS
WAY

ART NOUVEAU

Art Nouveau was an artistic movement characterised by the use of highly stylised organic motifs, especially ones inspired by plants. As such, the typefaces of the time were very often flowing and elegant.

Art-nouveau type often has embellished stroke endings and makes good use of ascenders and descenders, so you can really go to town on the detail. The style always makes me think of the metro in Paris.

As you can see in my examples below, I have added organic swirls and a heavier weight to the stroke ends at the bottom of the characters.

Arnold Böcklin

Arnold Böcklin is one of the most popular and recognisable art-nouveau typefaces, named after the Swiss symbolist painter.

This is a display typeface, so it's not ideal for body copy, but great for elaborate headings and titles.

TRY CREATING SOME OF YOUR OWN ART-NOUVEAU TYPE

WHY NOT TRY...
Using the background pattern of this page to create your letterforms?

USE THIS STYLE WHEN...

You want to add a little decadence to your hand-drawn words. It works very nicely with illustrations too.

BAUHAUS

You have most likely heard of Bauhaus,
the revolutionary art school in Germany.
It taught typography as part of the
curriculum and advocated sans serif
type, due to its simple geometric form.

The school influenced the arts, architecture, product design
and graphic design in the 20th century; its emphasis was on
the harmony between form and function.

There are lots of typographic posters by Bauhaus, or posters
influenced by the school. With my poster in progress to the
right, showing the sequence of creating the word 'Bauhaus',
I have started to look at how geometric shapes can make
up the type characters. As you can see, the word is created
simply out of triangles, squares and circles.

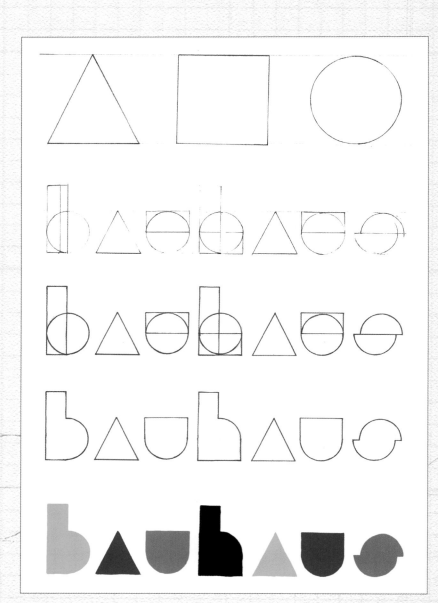

TRY CREATING SOME OF YOUR
OWN BAUHAUS·INSPIRED TYPE

WHY NOT TRY...

Creating your own Bauhaus posters?

SAUL BASS (1920–1996)

Saul Bass, one of my favourite graphic designers, worked on many film posters and title sequences during his illustrious career (you will have seen his work if you're a fan of Alfred Hitchcock films). He also designed numerous iconic corporate logos.

His style was distinctive and minimalistic, combining a hand-drawn typographic feel with simple graphic illustration to great effect. He pretty much revolutionised title credits in films by making them part of the whole cinematic experience.

I have created my own type-and-graphic illustration below, as a nod towards some of his work.

**TRY CREATING SOME OF YOUR
OWN SAUL BASS-INSPIRED TYPE**

WHY NOT TRY...
Using your favourite movie title as a starting point?

USE THIS STYLE WHEN...
The word alone is not enough. Hand-drawn
type combined with a simple illustration
can be very striking.

THREE-DIMENSIONAL

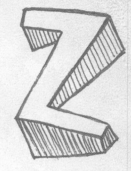

There are a million and one ways you can draw three-dimensional type. It became very popular for advertisements and signs in the 1800s (see page 96), but has survived through the years.

You can get really creative with how you give dimension to your type. You can be playful and create visual illusions like the 'R' at the top of this page: it feels like it's sinking into the paper, while the 'Z' uses an impossible perspective.

1

2

3

4

PLAYING WITH THE NEGATIVE SPACE

With the letter 'A' above, I originally started out drawing all the parts that make up the three-dimensional effect. But as I worked it up I thought I would start to take away some of the lines, and allow the eye to fill in the missing parts.

TRY CREATING SOME OF YOUR OWN THREE-DIMENSIONAL TYPE

WHY NOT TRY...

Different shading techniques to fill in your shadows?

CLASSIC BOTTLE CAPS

I stumbled across the idea of collecting old bottle caps while researching for this book. They can be a great source of retro type inspiration.

With such a limited amount of space, you can see why it's so important for a brand to get their logo lettering right. It's also quite a challenge to draw type so small, so here is a chance for you to try (there are a couple of larger ones for you to practise on too). It really makes you think about the space you have and how the type can work within it.

Don't get too hung up on getting your caps perfect - treat them as rough ideas like I have below. You can always work up your favourite later.

TRY CREATING SOME OF YOUR OWN BOTTLE-CAP TYPE

N·R·G

WHY NOT TRY...
Sketching the branding of your favourite bottled drinks?

GED PALMER

Ged Palmer is a lettering artist and sign painter based in London.

With over 12 years' experience of working with letterforms, Ged offers typography, calligraphy, lettering and sign painting to discerning clients in the UK and abroad. His work has been recognized by the International Society of Typographic Designers, the Type Directors Club, and various publications worldwide. Today his work is mostly focused on the interplay of contemporary lettering with traditional sign painting and gold-leaf gilding.

www.gedpalmer.com

GED'S APPROACH

Ged was commissioned to design and paint a gilded door panel for a taxidermy shop in Manchester. The client asked for an ornate, early-20th-century-style piece that echoed the style of gold-leaf glass signs of that era.

He says: 'For the lettering I took inspiration from early sign-painting books and American ephemera. The compact lettering was chosen to make maximum use of the space in a portrait composition and the 'W's were elaborated to draw the eye to the relationship between the words. The 3D drop shadow was the final touch to make the lettering the focal point of the piece.'

TRY OUT YOUR OWN ORNATE SIGN TYPE ON THE NEXT PAGE ➡

GED PALMER [121]

WHY NOT TRY...

Framing some of your type
with a decorative outline?

FUTURISTIC
TYPE

EVEN THOUGH THE VERY IDEA OF
BEING FUTURISTIC DOESN'T REALLY
FIT WITH USING OLD-FASHIONED
TOOLS LIKE A PENCIL OR PEN, IT'S
SURPRISING HOW IT CAN INSPIRE
THE BEGINNINGS OF YOUR
HAND-DRAWN CREATIONS.

PIXEL TYPE

Pixels are normally associated with computers and electronic screen displays, but they can also provide inspiration for an interesting hand-drawn type style.

Bitmap type on a screen consists of a fixed matrix of dots (pixels) that defines the shape and size of each character in the typeface.

Therefore, a good way to start experimenting with pixel typefaces is to use graph paper to help you draw.

SOME LITTLE POINTERS

Draw out the outline of your type, making sure you have enough height to allow for all characters.

Once you are happy with the outline, you can start to fill in the characters and see how it looks.

You can always block out your pixel typeface in a solid black to give a different feel. You could change the weight of the characters by halving the pixels.

YOU CAN CREATE NEW STYLES BASED ON THE PIXEL FORMAT

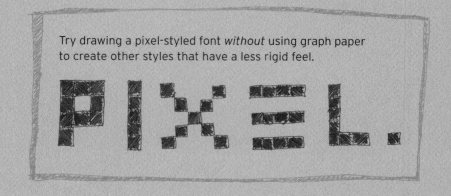

Try drawing a pixel-styled font *without* using graph paper to create other styles that have a less rigid feel.

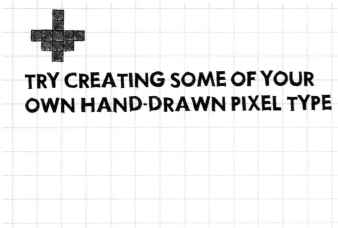

TRY CREATING SOME OF YOUR
OWN HAND-DRAWN PIXEL TYPE

RUH

ISOMETRIC TYPE

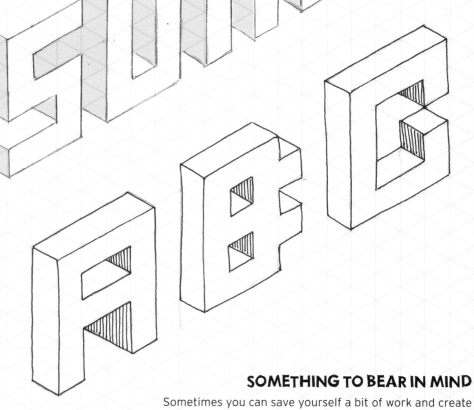

Building on the idea of pixel type (see page 126), you can create square-looking characters with added depth using an isometric grid.

Isometric projection is used in technical drawings to show three-dimensional objects in two dimensions, and can be used to great effect with type.

As you can see, I've started to create my own isometric type here. There are endless options: you can get really complex or simplify things right down and create some minimal type.

SOMETHING TO BEAR IN MIND

Sometimes you can save yourself a bit of work and create more than one character while you're working on your type. See below how an 'A' can easily become an 'M'.

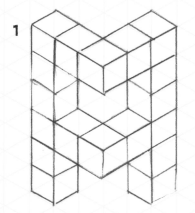

1

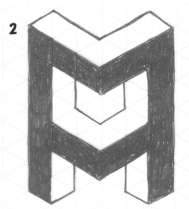

2

3

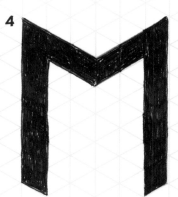

4

**TRY CREATING SOME OF
YOUR OWN ISOMETRIC TYPE**

NEON

This approach is interesting, because the very nature of neon type doesn't really lend itself to being hand-drawn!

Nevertheless, it's a really nice theme to work with to influence the look and feel of your type.

Neon signs are created using tubes of neon light – sometimes curly, sometimes straight – which means the letterforms they make are fragmented and tentative. Keep this in mind when sketching your neon-inspired type.

LIGHT

LICHT

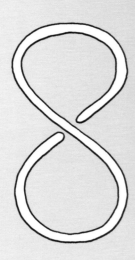

TRY CREATING SOME OF
YOUR OWN NEON TYPE

WHY NOT TRY...
Sketching words related to light, such as 'bright' or 'glow', in a neon style?

SHEDDING SOME LIGHT ON THE TYPOGRAPHIC SITUATION

If you want to light up your hand-drawn creations, you can always scan and manipulate them on your computer, as I have here.

ELECTRIC

I first played with LED lights in science class at school – little did I know that one day I would be creating type inspired by them!

Even though they've been around for years, LEDs have a futuristic vibe. To create this style you'll need to work to a grid, such as when sketching out pixel type (see page 126). You could even create some illustrative icons to go with your type. In my example below, I was thinking of the typical red LED bulbs, hence my choice of colour. I've also added a hint of light to give a three-dimensional feel.

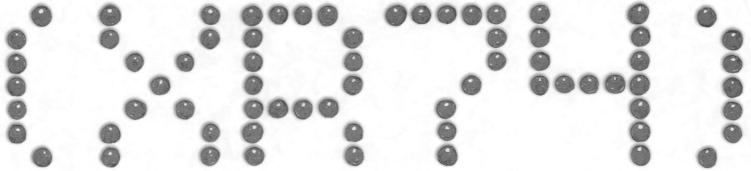

TRY CREATING SOME OF YOUR
OWN ELECTRIC-INSPIRED TYPE

LIGHTEN UP

As with your neon type (page 134), if you want to light up your hand-drawn creations, you can scan them and manipulate on your computer as I have here.

GOT A WHITE PEN?

CIRCUIT BOARD

Inspiration for your hand-drawn type can come from anywhere, so why not the inside workings of your Mac or PC?

Printed circuit boards are a maze of connecting lines and have a real futuristic feel. Find some images online (or use the real thing if you have it!) and try working the patterns into your own type characters, or take elements to be your starting point.

You can make your circuit-board-inspired type really complex or as minimal as you like. I have simplified my 'M' on the right by using one key line and two connectors at the beginning and the end.

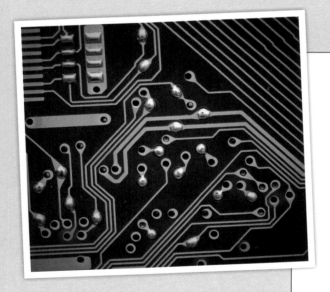

DEVELOPING YOUR CIRCUIT-BOARD TYPE

Even though my finished type looks very simple, it actually took quite a bit of thought. You can see how I started adding more connectors where the lines join. As I worked out how the letter would be drawn though, I started to take lines away, as I felt it was getting too busy.

A little tip for you with this one: use a ruler!

1  2

3  4

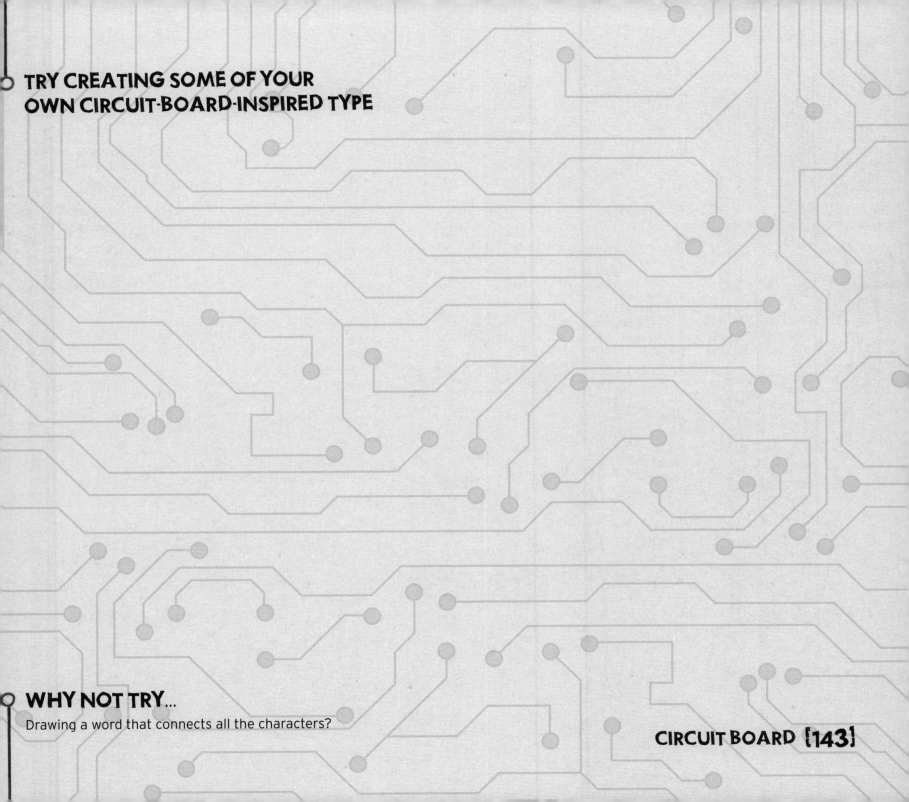

TRY CREATING SOME OF YOUR OWN CIRCUIT-BOARD-INSPIRED TYPE

WHY NOT TRY...

Drawing a word that connects all the characters?

USE THIS STYLE WHEN…
You want a highly technological feel for your hand-drawn type.

ANDREI ROBU

Andrei Robu is a design director specialising in type and brand identity. He's also pursuing his painting passion, combining what he learned as a graffiti artist with the craft of calligraphy.

With almost 15 years of experience as a graphic designer, Robu has worked with some big names of the corporate world. His work is recognised by many international publications and has been featured in exhibits around the world. Robu is also known for founding and curating the online typography gallery Typeverything.

www.robu.co

ANDREI'S APPROACH

Andrei was commissioned to create a type-based artwork around the theme of effective and original typefaces. His fragmented, overlapping letterforms give the impression of deconstructed type and design in progress, but at the same time the lettering seems coherent. The intersecting lines, thick and thin strokes, and geometric shapes give a definite modernist feel to the type.

Andrei says: 'I wanted to portray the idea of designing a typeface from a starting sketch to a finished artwork, and try to incorporate the feel of measuring up and structure.'

TRY OUT YOUR OWN DECONSTRUCTED TYPE ON THE NEXT PAGE

ANDREI ROBU {147}

WHY NOT TRY...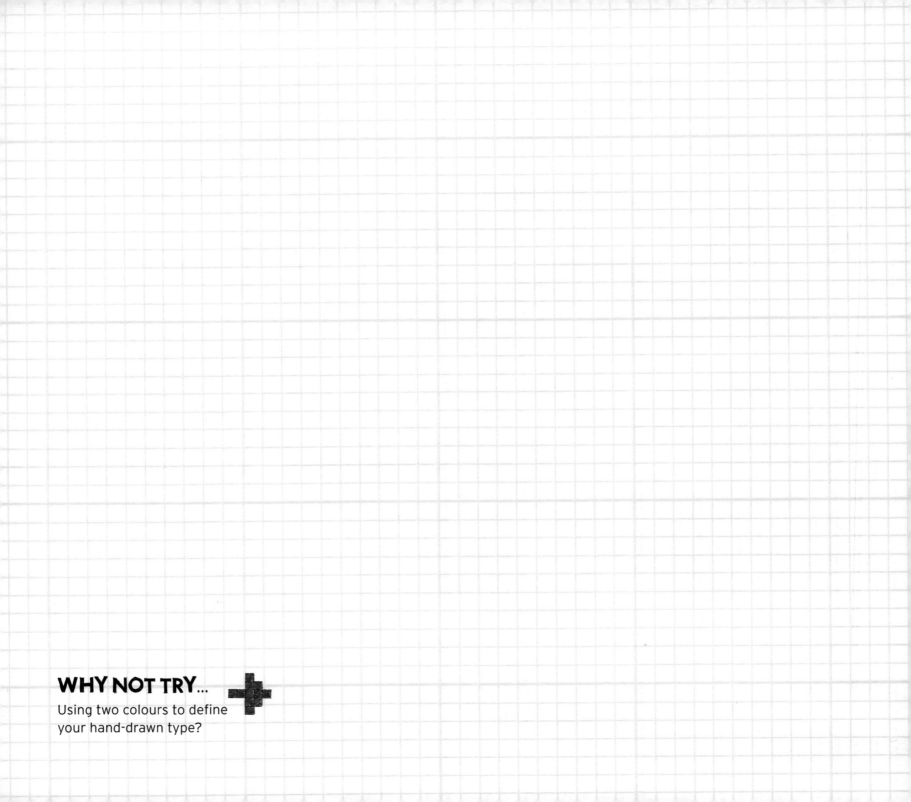

Using two colours to define
your hand-drawn type?

ORNAMENTAL
TYPE

THIS SECTION LOOKS AT THE
MORE DECORATIVE SIDE OF
SKETCHING TYPE.

BY INCORPORATING DRAWING
AND DOODLING INTO YOUR
LETTERS, YOU CAN CREATE
ORIGINAL AND
UNIQUE-LOOKING TYPE.

ALL THE FUN OF THE FAIR

Funfairs were big in the 19th century (and occasionally are today), which explains why the type used to advertise the attractions is almost always eye-catching and elaborate.

Electric light bulbs were also invented in the 19th century, which helped make funfair signs look even more impressive.

I have used light bulbs as the inspiration for my funfair-themed type below. On the right you'll see another example, where I used intricate patterns to fill in the characters: the options are endless! Just remember to keep it fancy.

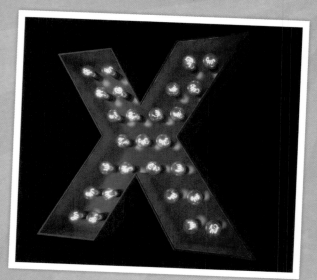

TRY CREATING SOME OF
YOUR OWN FUNFAIR TYPE

DROP IT

Drop caps - capital letters that drop below the line of type they start on - have been around in typography since the 5th century.

They can be extremely decorative characters, like the traditional illuminated styles found in manuscripts of the Middle Ages (see right). Equally, they can be simplistic and modern, geometric or quirky - it's really up to you!

You can incorporate any kind of stylistic elements into your drop cap letters, making them great for introducing a theme to your type.

TRADITIONAL ILLUMINATED DROP CAP

TRY MIXING UP YOUR OWN DROP CAPS

WHY NOT TRY...
Writing the opening line of your favourite book with a drop cap?

DROP IT 〔157〕

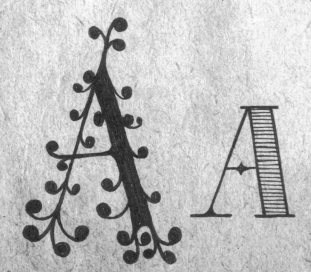

USE THIS STYLE WHEN...
You want to create a decorative
focal point on a page of type.

NATUREBETS

All you need to do to find inspiration for a naturebet is to sit in your garden or go for a walk in the park!

There is a history of introducing floral motifs into typography, dating back to early Greek and Latin texts. The leaf-shaped 'fleuron' glyph is one of the oldest typographical dingbats (see page 78).

But it needn't stop there. You can find lots of other things in nature to get your imagination going: everything from water, wildlife, insects or even the weather.

TRY CREATING YOUR OWN NATUREBETS

WHY NOT TRY...
Creating a naturebet using real leaves?

THE AMPERSAND

The ampersand (&) is typographic shorthand for the word 'and'. It can be a very elegant character and comes in handy to save space, so you often see it being used in logos.

The traditional ampersand takes the shape of the letters 'e' and 't' (et), which is Latin for the word 'and'. You can see this shape in the example to the right.

Ampersands can be highly stylised and idiosyncratic, meaning you can find some very quirky-looking examples in existing typefaces. This is a great place to look for inspiration.

NICE LITTLE EXTRAS
Why not incorporate some icons into your ampersand to give them an extra bit of character?

TRY CREATING SOME OF YOUR OWN AMPERSANDS

WHY NOT TRY...

Using an ampersand to join the names of a famous duo?

USE THIS STYLE WHEN...
You want to create a focal point within
a pair of words you're joining up.

SKETCHING BRANDS

You can learn a lot from sketching the typographic logos of the big brands. They have spent time and money getting them right over the years, often tweaking them along the way. The type used can be very stylised, to help with the brand recognition.

Brand identities that use only styled type are also known as wordmarks. Although, if you look carefully at the FedEx wordmark to the right, you will see a hidden icon in the negative space - a cheeky little touch that points you in the right direction, so to speak!

TRY DRAWING SOME OF YOUR FAVOURITE WORDMARK LOGOS

WHY NOT TRY...

Sketching a different word using an existing brand lettering style?

DOODLETYPE

We all like to doodle every now and then. I do it a lot when I'm finding it hard to focus on a job I actually need to get on with.

Luckily for me, I got to doodle all over this page for a reason: to give you ideas for your own doodletype!

You can start with random doodles and then work them into a letter shape - or start with a letter and doodle inside it. You might stumble across a formula that could be the start of a whole new typeface.

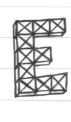

**TRY DRAWING SOME OF
YOUR OWN DOODLETYPE**

USE THIS STYLE WHEN...
You want to add playful, humorous
elements to your type.

ABCDe

MIX IT UP

Mixing up type styles takes a bit of thought and experimentation. It can be tricky to get right, but when you do, it looks great.

The key is to choose styles that create a nice contrast – but not so much that they look disjointed. It's really important to get the various sizes and negative spaces to look right.

When sketching my 'Stop, Look & Draw' phrase, I had to try to get the last two words to sit with the first two, so I opted for an ampersand. This not only helped me to keep the type as a nice unit visually, it also allowed me to add another level of contrast by using a logogram (&) and a ligature (ra).

TRY MIXING UP YOUR OWN STYLES

WHY NOT TRY...

Mixing up the styles in a single word like I have here?

JAMIE CLARKE

Based in Australia, Jamie draws illustrative type and lettering.

His eye-catching typography brings stories to life with imagery and decoration. After ten years of running his own digital agency, working with many globally recognised clients, Jamie decided to retrain. He studied Type Design in the Department of Typography at Reading University, and Letterpress at the St. Bride Foundation in London.

www.jamieclarketype.com

TRY OUT YOUR OWN
TYPE DECORATION
ON THE NEXT PAGE

JAMIE'S APPROACH

Jamie set out to design a set of
ampersands based on the work of
type founder Louis John Pouchée.

He says: 'When applying decoration
to letters there's a danger the
combination can look complex or
messy. I find it best if my decoration
follows a simple pattern or has some
symmetry that's in harmony with the
letter shape.

Regardless of how detailed the final
design might be, I find it important
to draw a simple underlying structure
within the letter that helps the eye
easily comprehend the whole design.'

JAMIE CLARKE [181]

WHY NOT TRY...

Designing the letter of your first name,
decorating it with personal details?

FUN 6 TYPE

THIS SECTION IS ABOUT
HAVING FUN WHEN YOU'RE
SKETCHING TYPE!

EXPERIMENTING WITH DIFFERENT
APPROACHES AND DRAWING
IMPLEMENTS IS PART OF FINDING
NEW STYLES FOR YOUR TYPE.

DOT-TO-DOT

I loved tackling dot-to-dot colouring books as a kid – especially making sure I kept the felt-tip fills within the lines. Obviously I was destined to become a graphic designer.

Dot-to-dot type can take a bit of planning to get right. As with pixel type (see page 126), you need to allow enough height in your initial characters to accommodate the various traits of the other characters in your word. Letters such as 'B', 'E' and 'R' are good to start with, as they need more height for the horizontal strokes to be drawn.

As you can see to the right, I've added and taken away parts of the type, each time creating the unique beginnings of a potential dot-to-dot type alphabet.

TRY CREATING SOME OF
YOUR OWN DOTTY TYPE

RIP IT UP

For this one you will need a sheet of paper. I've used white, but you can use pretty much any colour or any kind.

To help create your ripped-up type you can draw a rough guide on your paper before you start ripping out the letters, or, as I have, just jump straight in and start tearing out the words – it's fun!

This isn't sketching in the traditional sense, but you're still shaping type, just with paper and not a pen or pencil. Just remember not to go too small with your characters, otherwise you won't be able to achieve the detail (counter-less type is a good option too).

CREATING A HAND-DRAWN STYLE FROM YOUR PAPER CREATIONS

As you can see above, you can always make a new type style using your paper type as inspiration.

**TRY CREATING SOME OF YOUR OWN
RIPPED TYPE AND STICK IT IN HERE**

WHY NOT TRY...
Freestyling with scissors to create some cut-out type?

CONTINUOUS LINE

This one doesn't really need any preliminary sketching or planning – you just need to start drawing.

If you make a mistake sketching this style, it doesn't matter! The idea is to keep your line going – re-drawing the character several times over to build up the effect – without lifting your pen or pencil from the paper.

I prefer the pen approach when doing this, because you have to stick with the initial marks you put down on the paper – once you start there is no going back!

TRY CREATING SOME OF YOUR
OWN CONTINUOUS TYPE

WHY NOT TRY...
Drawing some script-style letters with a continuous single line?

123

C-60

Being a child of the 1980s, I grew up recording the Top 40 music charts on a Sunday evening with C-60 cassette tapes. I would spend hours writing out the track listings and illustrating the covers.

For this exercise, though, I thought it would be a nice challenge to create a continuous word using the actual tape as inspiration.

If you tried making a word out of the tape itself it would curl and twist, giving the impression of different widths, as you can see in my example to the right. A very interesting style!

TRY CREATING SOME OF YOUR OWN CASSETTE-TAPE TYPE

WHY NOT TRY...
Sketching the titles of your favourite songs or artists in tape type?

C-60 [199]

STRETCH IT

You can double the width, halve the height, squeeze and pull your type around to create new styles from existing ones, or to mix and match your letters.

In the example below I've used my daughter's name, Matilda, to show how you can combine exaggerated styles to create a unique-looking piece of type. We touched on the subject of type weight earlier (see page 36), but this takes the idea to another level.

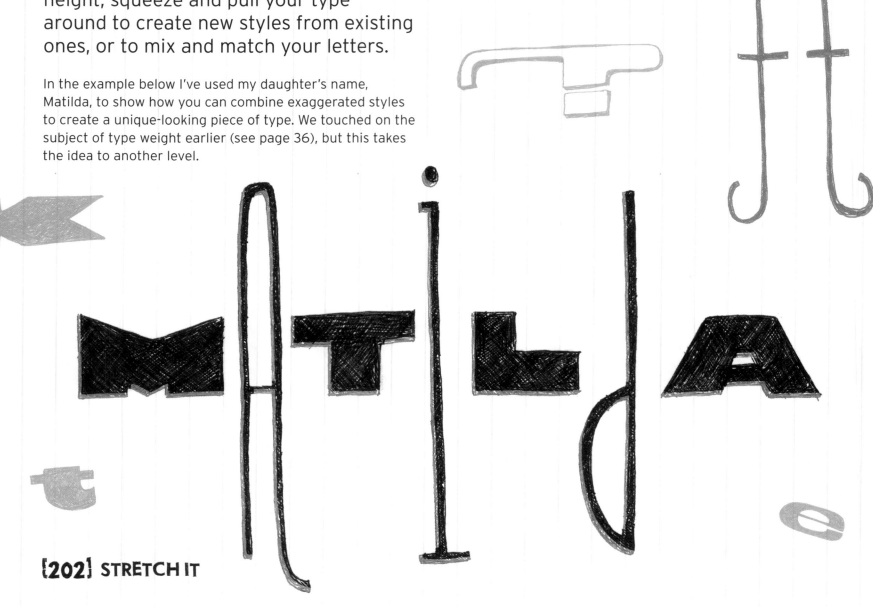

TRY STRETCHING SOME
OF YOUR TYPE AROUND

WHY NOT TRY...

Sketching the word 'stretch' in different ways?

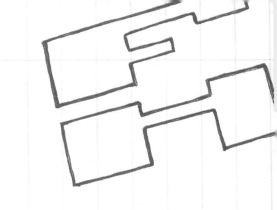

USE THIS STYLE WHEN...
You want to give your type an abstract,
quirky look. It's not the most legible way
to draw type, but it can look cool!

ILLUSTRATED

Combining illustration with type is a great way of adding a whole new dimension to your lettering.

For my type illustration I chose the subject of eating. I came up with a relevant word and started thinking about how it could be drawn to reflect the concept. I felt the type needed to be bulky in style, which gave me plenty of surface area to get my teeth stuck into.

I kept the type simple to allow the illustrated elements to stand out. Adding the three-dimensional effect at the end really helped emphasise the bite mark.

1

START WITH A ROUGH SKETCH

With a sketch you can see very quickly if your idea will work – if it looks bad it's easy to rub out and start again! You can see in step 1 (above) that I included an eye-shaped counter in the 'e', but in the end I felt the eye connection was too much, so at step 2 (below), I lost it.

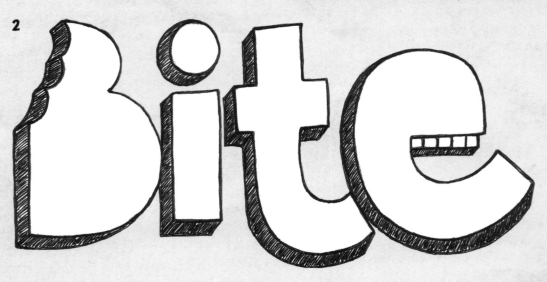

2

TRY CREATING SOME OF
YOUR OWN ILLUSTRATED TYPE

THE DEVIL IS IN THE DETAIL...

Try finding visual links between the characters and the word you're drawing.

RuN + h·de

TYPOGRAPHIC FILLS

Typographic fills are a variation on illustrated type (see page 206), except here the illustration determines how the type is drawn.

In my example, I have created a multilingual typographic image using the word 'hand'. You can see how I've drawn the type to fit the shape, and used initial caps to help separate the words.

You can create any shape you think of to fill with your hand-drawn type. Here I used words that relate to the shape, but that's for you to decide...

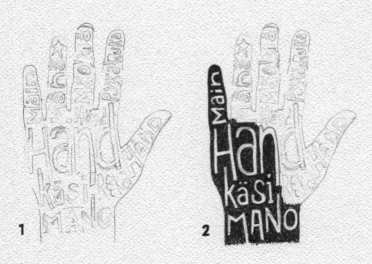

1

2

3

TRY CREATING YOUR OWN TYPOGRAPHIC FILLS

WHY NOT TRY...

Sketching your type to fit a given shape without using an outline as a guide?

USE THIS STYLE WHEN...
You want the emphasis to be on your illustration, rather than your type.

MICHELLE THORP

Michelle Thorp is a Kiwi illustrator living in Australia.

Her style is a mix of influences such as Jhonen Vasquez's *Invader Zim*, the 1930s-inspired Mcbess and the abundantly detailed vector styling of JThree Concepts. Michelle's work often consists of flat, varying line weights, sharp geometric shapes, handmade type and highly saturated colours. Her main focus is vector art, branding, character, logo, type, icon and textile design.

www.behance.net/michelleevelyn

MICHELLE'S APPROACH

This typographical play on words is based around a common social media theme: 'likes' – specifically, the aim of getting 100 likes. The joke is that here the word is confused with 'licks'. As you can see, the '100' is made up of zombie heads and a limb – you wouldn't expect these guys to know the difference between 'likes' and 'licks', would you?! So the type zombies fit the theme.

As this was also a vectored piece, the text needed to complement the clean-cut line work of the zombie characters without being lost among the detail.

MICHELLE THORP [215]

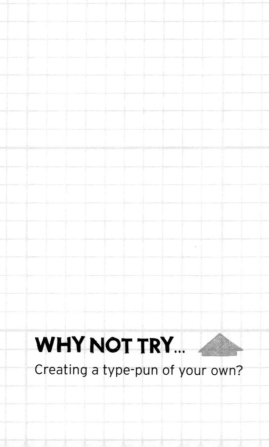

WHY NOT TRY...

Creating a type-pun of your own?

USING YOUR TYPE

The great thing about creating your own hand-drawn type is that no one else can use it! It doesn't exist as a font on a computer and its has your own individual quirks.

You could start using some of your styles to create labels for your home brew beer. Why not add an extra touch of class to the homemade marmalade you are going to be giving as presents for Christmas, you can even personalise it!

You don't have to stick to using a pen and pencil, try using objects and photograph your type or try cooking up a typographic treat!

HOME BREW BOTTLE LABELS

BIRTHDAY CARD STAMP

HOMEMADE FOOD LABELS

MIX UP YOUR STYLES

freeStyLe

MESSAGES IN THE SAND

DINNER PARTY MENU

DESIGN YOUR OWN TATTOO

BAKE YOUR OWN ALPHABET

ADD SOME EXTRA LOVE

USE ODD SOCKS

TYPE EMBROIDERY

DESIGN YOUR OWN T-SHIRT

PAINT YOUR WALLS

OMG! wtf?

MAKE A LETTER STAMP

HAVE YOUR OWN DOOR NUMBER

Salut Olà Ciao
Hej Tere Ni hao
Bonjour Holà
Привет Hello Selam
Ni hao Ciao
Salut Guten Tag
Hei Holà Olà

CUSTOM GREETING CARD DESIGN

TYPE ORNAMENTS

i ♥ type

NATURE is my HOME

DRAW TYPE YOUR PHOTOGRAPHS

TYPE RESOURCES

This book is just the tip of the hand-drawn-type iceberg. If you're looking for more information about typography in general, or more examples of the hand-drawn variety, here are a few websites that might help:

TYPOGRAPHY SITES

www.typographydeconstructed.com

www.welovetypography.com

www.fonts.com/content/learning

www.typographica.org

www.incredibletypes.com

www.typecooker.com

www.typedia.com

www.practicaltypography.com

HAND-DRAWN TYPE SITES

www.cargocollective.com/search/hand-drawn-type

www.theartofhandlettering.tumblr.com

www.typeverything.com

www.friendsoftype.com

OTHER SITES THAT MIGHT COME IN HANDY

www.dafont.com

www.skillshare.com

www.pinterest.com

 AND OF COURSE, YOU CAN ALWAYS JUMP ONTO GOOGLE AND DO AN IMAGE SEARCH!

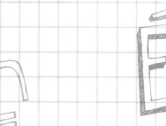

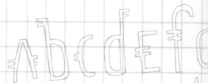

AUTHOR / DESIGNER / ILLUSTRATOR

LEE SUTTEY COMPLETED HIS DEGREE IN ILLUSTRATION AT THE UNIVERSITY OF PORTSMOUTH, GAINING A 1ST CLASS BA(HONS). HE THEN CONTINUED HIS EDUCATION WITH A MASTERS IN SEQUENTIAL DESIGN AND ILLUSTRATION AT THE UNIVERSITY OF BRIGHTON, BEFORE GOING ON TO WORK FOR VARIOUS MULTIMEDIA AND GRAPHIC DESIGN AGENCIES. HE NOW WORKS AS A FREELANCE GRAPHIC DESIGNER FOR PRINT AND SCREEN UNDER THE NAME VISUAL FUNCTION_.

LEE HAS ALSO TAKEN PART IN A TOURING EXHIBITION WITH HIS ARTIST BOOK WORK CALLED 'CHANGING PAGES', CURATED BY THE COLLINS GALLERY.

HE LOVES USING HIS SKETCHBOOKS AND DRAWING TO GENERATE IDEAS, AND THIS IS WHERE HIS LOVE OF HAND-DRAWN TYPE ORIGINATED.

WWW.VISUALFUNCTION.CO.UK

CREDITS

p. 28 © GLYPHstock - Shutterstock

pp. 48/49 © Carl Fredrik

p. 74 © ChiccoDodiFC - Shutterstock

p. 86 © Margaret Cusack. Hand stitching by Janet Lombardo

p. 96 © Ghost signs - Getty

p. 108 © Movie Poster Image Art - Getty

p. 116 © cristi180884 - Shutterstock

pp. 120/121 © Ged Palmer

p. 134 Moulin Rouge image © atm2003 - Shutterstock; café image © 360b - Shutterstock

p. 138 © VikaSuh - Shutterstock

p. 142 © repbone - Shutterstock

p. 146 © Andrei Robu

p. 152 © antonsav - Shutterstock

p. 156 © Tom Grundy - Shutterstock

p. 180 © Jamie Clarke

p. 214 © Michelle Thorp

p. 218 Beer bottle © Kirill Z - Shutterstock; Letter stamp © Scott Suttey

p. 219 Food jars © Aneta_Gu - Shutterstock; pizza © hoverfly - Shutterstock; knuckles © Charles Knox - Shutterstock; sand © design36 - Shutterstock

p. 220 Baked alphabet © NinaM - Shutterstock; Big P © Ron Ellis - Shutterstock; heart © Filipe Frazao - Shutterstock; T-shirt © Who is Danny - Shutterstock; sock S © lipik - Shutterstock; type embroidery © Africa Studio - Shutterstock

p. 221 OMG © B & T Media Group Inc - Shutterstock; sticky R © Ron and Joe - Shutterstock; door number © Maor Winetrob - Shutterstock; greeting card © Vlada Young - Shutterstock; nature image © Aysezgicmeli - Shutterstock

p. 223 Lee's portrait © Daniel Palmer